Awake to Your Destiny

Volume 1

The Mind of Christ

Apostle Nadine Manning

Awake to Your Destiny

Volume 1

"The Mind of Christ"

ISBN 978-0-9898369-0-6

Printed in USA by Prophetic in Warfare Deliverance and Worship Tabernacle in association with Kingdom Graphics Designo Inc.

P.O. Box 343, Millville New Jersey 08332.
piwfm2000@comcast.net

Contents

This is Your Set Time of Favor

You may have given up on your purpose, vision, ministry, children or even believing in yourself or God. There are a few also, reading this page that have gotten discouraged because you had shared your dreams with someone who told you that it was not possible. You may have wanted validation from your leader or someone you looked up to move into your destiny. You may have even gotten discouraged to the point where you begin to spend your time money and service doing something that does not maximize your potential. Well this book is for you as a clarion call to "Awake to Your Destiny". I decree and declare that now is your set time of favor.

Gratefulness

To My Husband, Richard Manning, thank you for believing in me. Your prayers and support made this possible.

I also dedicate this book to my children Abigail, Aaron, Nathaniel and Joshua who are a product and testimony of truly being "Awakened to Your Destiny".

When doctors said no, Jesus say YES! After two miscarriages in 2004, one year later came forth three bundles of joy all at once and then Joshua soon after.

I had to keep my mind on Christ to keep on believing God for my miracles.

Foreword

First I would like to thank our Lord and Savior Jesus Christ for giving Apostle Nadine Manning such a passion to help people to come into their God given destiny. I have known Apostle Manning for over fifteen (15) years and during these years she has demonstrated a steadfast love for God, ministry and people. She is very committed and faithful to God, her family and the people she serves. I have observed and seen her growth spiritually over the years. Her clarity and Apostolic unction has increased tremendously in revelation, wisdom and knowledge of the Word of God.

Apostle Nadine Manning is an anointed woman of God, powerful intercessor and is very serious about her walk with Christ and as a result she does not compromise the Word. She lives in her prayer closet spending hours daily on her face seeking the mind of Christ in order to fulfill the commission God has given to the disciples. Whatever the Lord tells her to say that's exactly what she does. She operates only under the leading and influence of the Holy Spirit.

Her life and ministry has helped my family and myself to be more conscious of our God given purpose and destiny. She assisted in shaping me to take on greater challenges. Apostle Nadine Manning has been divinely ordained and commissioned by God to write this book *"Awake to Your Destiny" – Volume 1 (The Mind of Christ)* to help believers understand that we were all predestined to have the mind of Christ and if we walk in the Spirit our destiny is unstoppable. This is the only way we can have access to the keys to the Kingdom.

We can have the mind of Christ only when we are completely submitted to God. As a result of abiding in Christ and His word abides in you, according to St. John 15 you can ask anything in His name and it shall be done. Apostle Manning gives several verses of scriptures as references to support what she has written in this book.

While reading this book you will certainly have a life changing experience as you go through it thoughtfully and prayerfully. Apostle Nadine Manning is desirous of seeing believers living like kingdom people and this can only be done when we have the mind of Christ. The mind of Christ allows us to have an intimate relationship with the Father God. I encourage you to let this book be a part of your library, it's a must buy!

Minister Louise Marcia Vickers
B.A. Guidance and Counseling
Clarendon, Jamaica W.I.

Introduction

Awake to Your Destiny

"Wake up! Strengthen what little remains, for even what is left is almost dead. I find that your actions do not meet the requirements of my God. 3 Go back to what you heard and believed at first; hold to it firmly. Repent and turn to me again. If you don't wake up, I will come to you suddenly, as unexpected as a thief" (Rev. 3:2-3).

Jesus Christ entered the world with tiny wrinkles and cries. He was wrapped in strips of cloth and took His first sleep in a bed made of straw or hay. Like all of us, He was subject to time and to parents. He grew to manhood in Roman-governing and occupied Palestine. He grew from a child with gentle hands into becoming strong and calloused in his father's [Joseph's] woodworking shop. He encountered and experienced great triumphs and disappointments as a man.

Jesus walked through the villages and cities, touching individuals, preaching to crowds, and training twelve disciples to carry on His work. While on business from place to place, every step or move people hounded Him, seeking to rid the world of His influence.

Finally, falsely accused and tried, He was condemned to a disgraceful death by crucifixion with foreign hands. His journey to crucifixion entails—spat upon, cursed, pierced by nails, and hung heavenward for all to ridicule. Jesus, the God-man, gave His life completely so that all might live.

As we focus on the theme scripture for this awesome book series "Awake to Your Destiny", Revelations 3:2, let us be reminded that the book of Revelation is a book of hope. John, the beloved apostle and eyewitness of Jesus, proclaimed that the victorious Lord would surely return to vindicate the righteous and judge the wicked. Most importantly, Revelation is also a book of warning. Chapter two to three reveals that, things were not as they should have been in the churches. Therefore, Christ called the leaders and members to commit themselves to live in righteousness, to arise and strengthen that which remains.

This book, "Awake to Your Destiny" will be written in volumes. This is Volume 1 sub-titled *"The Mind of Christ"*. These series can be used as a devotional, bible study for churches, a group within the church or just for inspiration, encouragement or revelation. It is for the ideal entrepreneur or future business owner.

To be awakened to our destiny we must develop and maintain a life in the Spirit. A life cultivated in the Spirit is through constant fellowship with the Holy Spirit that comes from not only His divine presence but most importantly from abiding in the Word of God.

Jesus is God's Son therefore, we can perfectly trust what He says. By trusting in the Lord, we can gain an open mind to understand God's message and fulfill his purpose and destiny in our lives. Remember, we can only please God if we are spiritually minded. Romans 8: 5 declares:-

> *"For those who live according to the flesh set their minds on the things of the flesh, but those who live according to the Spirit, the things of the Spirit. 6 For to be carnally minded is death, but to be spiritually minded is life and peace."*

We are in a season of restoration and revival in the body of Christ where God is raising up a remnant with a mind to work. God is awakening the church to their destiny. It is a call to action and a state of vigilance. There is an awakening coming to the body of Christ as God is releasing a remnant with fireproof faith that are prepared for opposition. A mind to work speaks to developing and maintaining a consistent walk of faith. Moreover, it means you have the mind of Christ.

If you are walking into the flesh you cannot effectively discern or understand the things of God. God cannot have a relationship with us in the flesh because He is Spirit. If we are in the flesh we cannot please God. When we choose to walk in the flesh we are just religious, having a form of godliness denying the power thereof. As the Romans 8:7-9 explains,

> *"Because the carnal mind is enmity against God; for it is not subject to the law of God, nor indeed can be. 8 So then, those who are in the flesh cannot please God. 9 But you are not in the flesh but in the Spirit, if indeed the Spirit of God dwells in you. Now if anyone does not have the Spirit of Christ, he is not His."*

Therefore, a life in the spirit is walking and earnestly desiring the things of the God. Life in the spirit is "Empowerment Zone". As you constantly walk in the Spirit you will "Awake to Your Destiny with the Mind of Christ."

While in Texas at the TD. Jakes leadership conference in April 2013, the Lord revealed to me in my devotion that there is a stirring of the Lord happening in the realm of the Spirit. This is the stirring of the Lord as He is raising up a people filled with the zeal of the Lord that will carry out great exploits. Daniel 11:32b declares, ***"But the people who know their God shall be strong, and carry out great exploits."*** As you read these chapters, may you be stirred with excitement to come alive and walk into your season and be awakened to your destiny.

My prayer for you is that your mind be caught up with the arousing and stirring of the Lord. Regardless of your circumstances like Daniel and the three Hebrews boys you will not bow. I pray that you will position yourself to be transformed and be *"Awakened to Your Destiny"* to a place of "ACTION".

Chapter 1

Spiritual Blessings

"Blessed be the God and Father of our Lord Jesus Christ, who hath blessed us with all spiritual blessings in heavenly places in Christ: 4 according as He hath chosen us in Him before the foundation of the world, that we should be holy and without blame before Him in love: 5 having predestinated us unto the adoption of children by Jesus Christ to Himself, according to the good pleasure of His will, 6 to the praise of the glory of His grace, wherein He hath made us accepted in the beloved" (Ephesians 1:3-6).

We were already predestined to have the mind of Christ, having chosen us before the foundation of this world to lavish us with all spiritual blessings: - Where? *"In heavenly places".* Therefore, being predestined means that it has been prearranged and destined for us to be His sons and daughters, to inherit all spiritual blessings in heavenly places. Predestined also means appointed, preordained or foreordained. God has decided long before we were formed in our mother's womb our divine and eternal destiny.

To obtain all the promises God has for us we have to be adopted into the beloved. St. John 1:12 explains that:

> *"But as many as received Him, to them gave ye power to become the sons of God, even to them that believe on his name: 13 which were born, not of blood, nor of the will of the flesh, nor of the will of man, but of God"*.

Accepting Jesus Christ into your life as Lord and Savior has given you the power, authority and ability to become regenerated. You have within you the capacity to be renewed, to be restored and to become an agent of change. In other words, someone is waiting for their pre-determined deliverance and release. It is the anointing that has been invested [pre-determined] inside of you. The key is to be awakened in your spirit to who you are. You are called unto a high calling in Jesus Christ.

Accepting Christ make us sons of God signifying a divine or new birth. It is the beginning process of transformation through the shed blood of Jesus Christ. Salvation began and became instant when you accept and confess Jesus Christ as your Lord and Savior.

Romans 10:9-10 says:-

> *"That if thou shalt confess with thy*
> *mouth the Lord Jesus, and shalt believe*
> *in thine heart that God hath raised him*
> *from the dead, thou shalt be saved.*
> *10 For with the heart man believeth*
> *unto righteousness; and with the mouth*
> *confession is made unto salvation."*

Believing in the death burial and resurrection of Jesus Christ grants you access to the throne of grace. Therefore, *"8 Verily I say unto you, whatsoever ye shall bind on earth shall be bound in heaven: and whatsoever ye shall loose on earth shall be loosed in heaven"* (Matthew 18:18). Having been adopted as sons of God gives us the same privilege and access to God the Father and the spiritual portals of heaven.

As the scripture declares, you have the authority to bind and lose. This will only happen with an individual or people that has submitted themselves to the power of the Holy Spirit. God has given authority to the church and we have to submit ourselves to God to exercise that authority. LET THE WORD OF GOD WORK INSIDE OF YOU. It is the Word that quicken you and awake you to your God given destiny **[Power + authority = release into your divine destiny]**. St. John 1 also says in verse 12 that, *"But as many as received him, to them gave*

He power to become the sons of God, even to them that believe on his name".

My brothers and sisters in Christ Romans 10:8 says (paraphrased), the Word is nigh you, in your mouth and in your heart. When your mind is renewed and transformed by the Word of the Lord, then your spirit man will begin to activate your faith to believe God. Not only to believe God, but also to believe in yourself, that you can do all things through Christ which strengthens you.

Whatever your mind conceives will be confessed or released with your mouth, Proverbs 18:21 says *"Death and life are in the power of the tongue, and those who love it will eat its fruit."* The church has been given dominion power. The shed blood of Jesus Christ, God's redemptive plan is still at work, through which He has given us the right and authority to rule on earth. Adam and Even sinned in the garden, thwarting God's original divine plan. Nonetheless, God sent His only Son as Galatians 3:13-14 explains:

> *"Christ hath redeemed us from the curse of the law, being made a curse for us: for it is written, Cursed is every one that hangeth on a tree: 14 that the blessing of Abraham might come on the Gentiles through Jesus Christ; that we*

might receive the promise of the Spirit through faith".

Adam and Eve were given dominion *"over the fish of sea, over the cattle, over all the earth and over every creeping thing that creeps on the earth. So God created man in His own image"* (Genesis 1:26-27a). Because of the sin of disobedience man was banished from the Garden of Eden. But thank God for the shed blood of Jesus Christ that brings restoration to our spiritual position and blessings in heavenly places. You have been given a choice. Similar to the challenge that Joshua declared to the people in Joshua chapter 24:15 saying,

> *"And if it seem evil unto you to serve the Lord, choose you this day whom ye will serve; whether the gods which your fathers served that were on the other side of the flood, or the gods of the Amorites, in whose land ye dwell: but as for me and my house, we will serve the Lord."*

The choices that you make affects your thought process and ultimately will determine the outcome of your destiny. Your thoughts determine your action. Your actions forms habits. These habits develop character. Our character dictates our destiny. After all you can recount the many deliverances, healing and blessings God has bestowed on you. The demonstration of God's mighty hand and gracious acts can be seen in your life. Now tell me, who or what doth hinder you from running this race with patience.

The Lord has proven Himself and kept His side of the covenant. Now He is calling on you to declare solemnly that you will recommit yourself of your own freewill to serve Him and be awakened to your destiny. You can't do business as usual. He is calling you into a relationship, for others into a higher place of worship that heals, strengthens and release you into High Destiny.

GRACIOUS FATHER, we thank you for the forgiveness you offer us through Jesus Christ. He took the curse of the law upon Himself so that we might be received into your Kingdom. We praise you for enabling people from all nations to enter your Kingdom. In Jesus Name Amen.

Chapter 2

The Mind

The Seat of Understanding

The mind denotes generally the seat of reflective consciousness, comprising the faculties' of perception and understanding those feelings. The mind judges and determines in any given situation. 1 Corinthians 2:16 declares that, ***"For who hath known the mind of the Lord, that He may instruct him? But we have the mind of Christ"***. Through our union with Christ, we have access to Christ's mind, Christ's divine thoughts, and Christ's counsel. Isaiah 40:13, 18, 22 and 23 says:-

> *"Who has directed the Spirit of the LORD, Or as His counselor has taught Him? Isaiah 40 reveals that there is no one that can be compared to the Lord. There is no equal for Him. 18To whom then will you liken God? Or what likeness will you compare to Him? 22 It is He who sits above the circle of the earth, and its inhabitants are like grasshoppers, who stretches out the*

heavens like a curtain, And spreads them out like a tent to dwell in. 23 He brings the princes to nothing; He makes the judges of the earth useless.

We can't know what the Lord is thinking except through the guidance of the Holy Spirit. We have insight into some of God's plans, thoughts and actions through the revelation given by the Holy Spirit. We have *"The Mind of Christ"* through fellowship and communion with Him. Spending quality time with Christ and remaining constant in the Word of God and worshiping and praying in the spirit shapes and develop the very mind of Christ in us. An intimate relationship with Christ comes only from spending time consistently in His Word.

Spending time with the Lord requires sacrifice. You will always know the mind of Christ [mind of the Spirit] as you seek Him and stay constant in the Word, yielding yourselves wholeheartedly to God. Philippians 2:5 reveals that, Jesus Christ humbled himself and willingly gave up His rights in order to obey God and serve people. When you are a yielded servant of Christ it reflects in your attitude. You serve out of love for the Lord and for others, not out of guilt or fear.

Your mind is the seat of your heart and soul, your entire being. The "mind" is known as the place where thinking takes place, as opposed to the "heart," where feelings are created. Isaiah 46:8-11 reveals that the nation of Israel has double standard in their mind and thinking. James 1:6-8 says,

> *"But let him ask in faith, nothing wavering. For he that wavereth is like a wave of the sea driven with the wind and tossed. 7 For let not that man think that he shall receive any thing of the Lord. 8 A double minded man is unstable in all his ways."*

This led them to be tempted and also waver between the Lord God and pagan gods.

> *"Remember this, and shew yourselves men: bring it again to mind, O ye transgressors. 9 Remember the former things of old: for I am God, and there is none else; I am God, and there is none like me, 10 Declaring the end from the beginning, and from ancient times the things that are not yet done, saying, My counsel shall stand, and I will do all my pleasure: 11 Calling a ravenous bird from the east, the man that executeth my counsel from a far country: yea, I have spoken it, I will also bring it to*

pass; I have purposed it, I will also do it."

Isaiah affirms the sole Lordship of God. God is unique in His knowledge and in His control for the future. God's consistent purpose is to carry out what He has planned. When we are tempted to pursue anything that promises pleasure, comfort, peace or security apart from God, we must remember our commitment to God.

The Renewing of the Mind

Romans 12:1-2 admonished us saying,

> *1 I beseech you therefore, brethren, by the mercies of God, that you present your bodies a living sacrifice, holy, acceptable to God, which is your reasonable service. + 2And do not be conformed to this world, but be transformed by the renewing of your mind, that you may prove what is that good and acceptable and perfect will of God.*

The scripture rightly tells us that if we refuse to be transformed by the renewing of our mind that God leaves us to our debased (reprobate) mind. Debase meaning corrupt or good-for-nothing mind. The idea of "mind" appears quite rarely in the Gospels. It is mostly in connection with the heart. For example, the imaginations of the heart (Luke 1:51).

> *"And even as they did not like to retain God in their knowledge, God gave them over to a debased mind, to do those things which are not fitting; 29 being filled with all unrighteousness, sexual immorality, a wickedness, covetousness, maliciousness; full of envy, murder, strife, deceit, evil-mindedness; they are whisperers, 30 backbiters, haters of God, violent, proud, boasters, inventors of evil things, disobedient to parents, 31 undiscerning, untrustworthy, unloving, unforgiving, unmerciful; 32 who, knowing the righteous judgment of God, that those who practice such things are deserving of death, not only do the same but also approve of those who practice them"* (Romans 1:28-29).

Surrender yourself to the Lord, asking Him to show you the way out of sin and into the light of His freedom and His love. Prayer, Bible study, and loving support of Christians in a Bible-believing church can help you gain the strength you need to resist these powerful temptations. If you are already deeply involved in any form of immoral behavior, seek help from a trustworthy, professional, Christian counselor or Pastor.

The only other use of the word "mind" in the Gospels comes in Jesus' great commandment: ***"You shall love the Lord your God with all your heart, and with all your soul, and with all your strength, and with all your mind"*** Compare (Matthew 22:37; Mark 12:30; Luke 10:27). In saying this, Jesus was quoting from Deuteronomy 6:5, but that verse does not have the phrase *"with all your mind."* In Mark, however, the questioner repeats Jesus' command, but with a word for "understanding" in place of the word for "mind" (Mark 12:33).

As humans we are shaped by our thoughts and we become what we think. The thought of the mind has something different from the spirit; it has the ability to understand and to reason, to think (1 Corinthians 14:14-19). It is the seat of intelligence. In other places, "mind" is used in a broader sense including all of a person's mental and moral processes (Romans 12:2; Ephesians 4:23). A human's actions come from the inclinations of his or her mind. Whether a person is good or evil depends on the state of the mind.

Life in the Spirit

The state of a person depends upon what or who controls the mind. Romans 8:6-7 speaks of a person's mind being controlled either by the flesh or by the Spirit. The person whose mind is controlled by the flesh is evil. The mind controlled by the Spirit leads to good. Other passages describe the inclination of a person's mind being controlled by the god of this world (2 Corinthians 4:4). People whose minds are controlled by the *"god of this world"* will have their minds darkened and will not be able to understand the world as it really is (2 Corinthians 3:14).

To be "Awaken to Your Destiny" requires us to *"walk in the spirit"*. This is a life controlled by the spirit of the Lord through a constant, abiding relationship with Jesus Christ. As the Holy Spirit is communicating by His Spirit through the pages of this awesome book "Awake to Your Destiny", He is ushering you in His abiding presence where you will live, move and have your being in the Glory. Many are still operating like a veil is still over their understanding. But the Lord can open people's minds. For example, Jesus opened the minds of the disciples who walked the Emmaus road with Him so that they could understand the Scriptures (Luke 24:45).

For Paul, conversion is considered to be a *"renewing of the mind"* (Romans 12:2; Ephesians 4:23). In both cases, the process is one in which God takes control of the mind of a person through the Holy Spirit and leads the thoughts of that person in the right direction. Thus, the renewed person is given the ability to know God's will. Such people have new minds and can make accurate or clear spiritual discernment (1 Corinthians 2:15-16).

Chapter 3

Going Beyond the Veil

God is calling us as a body of believers as well as those who have turn back from following Him to be restored and pursue Christ with a passion by going beyond the veil. Going beyond the veil is breaking through that mirror of your human reasoning, ideologies and yielding yourself totally to God's divine presence. Your true purpose and destiny will only emerge in this season as you press through in the secret place, going beyond the veil. Beyond the veil is a place where your thoughts become His thoughts and your ways are transformed to His ways.

Beyond the veil is a God-conscious mind set. Even though, we deal with earthly circumstances, decisions to be made as well as transitions that are inevitable in our lives, God's wisdom, peace and strength will be yours as you come back to *"A Heart of Worship"* where it is all about pleasing God. Telling Him, you are sorry for the things I've made it and *"it is all about you, it is all about you Jesus."* Going beyond the veil requires the faith factor which is vital, because it entails going beyond what is ordinary and doing something that is extreme.

- o Extreme means: Life-threatening, risky, also means exciting.
- o Reaching a high or the highest degree very great: not usual; exceptional;

When God calls you into the extreme, that is, *"Going Beyond The Veil"* it is going above and beyond. Everyone can't go with you and will not be able to go with you beyond the veil. It calls for separation. The veil was a curtain in the temple separating the Holy Place from the Most Holy Place (Exodus 26:31-33). According to Matthew's gospel the veil was torn from top to bottom at the time of Jesus' death. But we are walking and living with a mind-set as if the veil was not done away with.

Awake to your destiny is simply telling us ***"And be not conformed to this world: but be ye transformed by the renewing of your mind, that ye may prove what is that good, and acceptable, and perfect, will of God***
(Romans 12:2). Nothing can be concealed or disguised beyond the veil. Today, we qualify to be in God's presence not on the basis of rituals, but on the basis of our righteousness in Christ. We are all called to an intimate fellowship with God. To relate to Him through prayer is our birthright as adopted sons of the Father. However, communing with God at the deepest level requires that we become transformed. This

is only done through constant fellowship beyond the veil.

Seeing Through the Eyes of God

There is only one way to fulfill your destiny and maximize your potential and that is to see yourself through the eyes of God. Jeremiah was urged by God to pray to reveal matters concerning the future which are unknowable humanly. You can only see the vision of your purpose, life, ministry or specific divine assignment through the eyes of God. Only when you submerge yourself in His presence *"Going Beyond The Veil"* will you see through the eyes of God.

Maybe you have gone through a shameful experience such as being raped or molested. Or you may have been victimized and abused verbally, mentally or physically. Or like Hagar in Genesis chapter 21, you may have been forced against your will to carry someone else's vision or spiritual baby. You thought it was the right thing to do and you submitted to that leader and served faithfully. But like Hagar, you were rejected in spite of how you honestly and humble served. Now you are left to not only carry this baby but birth it out and nurture it.

Hagar, felt deserted, cast away, neglected and she was hurting. Your list maybe longer. But you are not alone and purpose cannot die. 1 Thessalonians 5:24 declares that, *"Faithful is he that calleth you, who also will do it."* She had to awake to her destiny and see herself through the eyes of God. If God deposited His Holy Spirit in you, in addition to that gave you a vision, then He will also make the provision. God is getting ready to turn things around. He is working all things for your good because you love Him and because you are called according to His purpose (Romans 8:28).

What God has for you is for you. He will bring you out of that place of shame, pain, turmoil and confusion into your destiny. Genesis 21:14 explains that Abraham prepared food for her and a container of water and strapped them on Hagar's shoulder and sent her away with the child. Genesis 21:14b – 15 reveals, *"She wandered aimlessly in the wilderness of Beersheba. 15 When the water was gone, she put the boy in the shade of a bush"*.

Do you feel like Hagar at times, as if you are wandering aimlessly in the wilderness, looking and seeking desperately for a breakthrough?

- When will my turmoil end?
- I thought I was on the right track?
- The place that I served faithfully, has become my worst nightmare;

- And now I am alone and can't see my way out.

Hagar hid the baby in the shade of bushes and walked away from it so she would not see it die of hunger and thirst (vs.15). Hagar *"burst into tears",* but God heard the cry of the baby. Listen, God hears the cry of the spiritual baby [the vision, the purpose, your destiny] crying inside of you! You are about to experience the SUDDENLIES OF GOD to awake you to your destiny. The Lord was on a quest to renew Hagar's mind so that she could see through His eyes the purpose and vision for her life.

Get ready for a divine visitation from heaven. Genesis 21:17a says, *"But God heard the boy crying, and the angel of God called to Hagar from heaven"*. Like Hagar, the Lord is reassuring you through the pages of this book, *"don't be afraid, He has heard your cry, don't abort your purpose, Awake to Your Destiny"*. At the point or when it seems like the way before you is dark and lonely, suddenly the Lord sends divine intervention.

Genesis 21:19 says, *"Then God opened Hagar's eyes, and she saw a well full of water. She quickly filled her water container and gave the boy a drink."* God hears your cry in your desperate search after Him beyond the veil. God is opening your eyes through these pages,

"Therefore with joy shall ye draw water out of the wells of salvation" (Isaiah 12:3).

The trials and storms of life you have experienced has caused you to remain hidden and appears to have pushed your purpose under the bushes but the Lord has *now "opened [your] eyes."* Had Hagar forgotten the promise (Genesis 16:11)? Whether she looked to God or not, He directed her to a fountain close by, probably hidden amid brushwood, and with this water she revived her dying son. God is redirecting and reviving your purpose or vision as you endeavor to go beyond the veil and – *"Awake to Your Destiny".*

Chapter 4

Uzziah Must Die

This is in line with the inspiration I received from an excerpt from Charles Jenkins book, "**Thriving in Change**". I heard the voice of the Lord spoke these word to me on February 25, 2013 around 12 noon, "Even though, in God our vision is already made, God depends on us as well as we need people to execute the strategy of the vision". Then I heard these word as well even as I write this chapter that *"My vision has been predestinated"*! Hallelujah, thank you Jesus. Your vision my brothers and sisters is unstoppable because God has predestined your vision before you were born. The Lord has also positioned people to help you.

During my devotion and worship with the Lord that same morning of February 25th, He showed me in an open vision that many have been trying to fulfill the vision He gave them through the eyes of their predecessors and those they admire. I kept praying in the spirit even the more. Then I heard the Lord spoke again from that open vision that so many are delayed from entering into everything God has for them because they are trying to fulfill the vision or dream through the eyes or vision of their predecessors.

Even though, these predecessors are or were great men and women who have encountered many victories, you will still be unable to come into everything God has for you because you have lost your focus. Similarly, the vision given to you will be short-lived if you do not willing submit and obey the voice of the Lord. It requires total obedience and submission to the vision, plan and purpose God has for your life to be *"Awakened to Your Destiny"* through the eyes of the God.

How many of us have taken our eyes off the Lord and trying to be like somebody else that you have admired? You have seen great successes through their ministry, their life as well as contribution to society. You then become stuck in your process because you are banking on their experiences only and what they have accomplished.

You have taken your eyes off the all-powerful, all knowing, all seeing God. But I hear the voice of the Lord saying, *"What has become an Uzziah in your life must die."* Isaiah 6:1-4, declares:-

> **"In the year that king Uzziah died I saw also the Lord sitting upon a throne, high and lifted up, and his train filled the**

temple. 2 Above it stood the seraphims: each one had six wings; with twain he covered his face, and with twain he covered his feet, and with twain he did fly. 3 And one cried unto another, and said, Holy, holy, holy, is the Lord of hosts: the whole earth is full of his glory. 4 And the posts of the door moved at the voice of him that cried, and the house was filled with smoke".

The vital lesson learned from this scripture is that when King Uzziah died, Isaiah was awaken to his destiny. Isaiah clearly depicts what this book is revealing to you *"Awake to Your Destiny".* Awake to a mind centered on Christ so you can experience His Glory and preclude your vision and dreams from becoming short lived.

When King Uzziah died three (3) things emerged or was awakened. First, when King Uzziah died Isaiah sought the Lord. Secondly, when King Uzziah died Isaiah searched his heart. Thirdly, when King Uzziah died Isaiah surrendered his life. Although, Uzziah was generally a good king with a long and prosperous reign, yet most of his people turned away from God.

Not only was he a good king but a successful king. He was a king who did what was right in the eyes of God. He served the tribe of Judah from the age of sixteen for 52 long years. During his time Judah became prosperous. He restored and rebuilt towns, had a well-trained powerful army, he produced great machinery and weapons. Apparently, Isaiah looked up to him with awe and respect. He had his eyes fixed on Uzziah because of his great accomplishments.

Uzziah became conceited and proud of his great accomplishments and he over emphasized his power. He thought that he could do everything and anything he wanted to do. He assumed that he could be a king and a priest at the same time by burning incense in the temple, which was the job of the priest and not the job of the king. God was displeased with what he had done and, because King Uzziah defiled the temple of God, God struck him with leprosy and later on he died.

Sometimes in order for us to get a proper view of who God is, somebody or something in our lives have to die. Usually, it is something or someone that we hold on to or look up to so dearly that keep us from seeing God for who He really is.

The question is what is your King Uzziah?

- Is it your boyfriend or girlfriend?

- Is it your job, car, house, family your job, drugs, liquor, or television shows.
- Or is it your health?

The other question is, what will it take for you to "Awake to your Destiny"?

It can be real simple and easy:

- Totally surrender to the Lord, and strengthen what remains.
- Return to what is most important that that is building on a firm foundation.
- Abiding in the Word of God, asking whatever you will and it shall be done.

Your mind is the seat of understanding God's good and perfect will for your life. Isaiah's mind was renewed and transformed when Uzziah died.

God is doing a new thing and we need to forget about the things we have done wrong and behold the Glory of the Lord to take us into our due season. Isaiah encounter with the Glory brought him to a place of humility and brokenness as he cried out to the Lord **"Woe is me! For I am undone; because I am a man of unclean lips, and I dwell in the midst of a people of unclean lips: for mine eyes have seen the King, the Lord of hosts"** (Isaiah 6:5). His understanding was enlightened to behold the Glory of the Lord. He went beyond the veil (Holy of Holies) and His mind conceived the idea that, even though I am a prophet and have been used by God during Uzziah's reign, there is more to my purpose and destiny than this.

The Lord spoke to Isaiah concerning his greater commission or assignment after he yielded himself in repentance. Yes, the next dimension was open to him after he yield himself totally to the Lord, forgetting the former things and beholding the new (beyond the veil). Isaiah *"heard the voice of the Lord saying, whom shall I send, and who will go for us? Then said I, Here am I; send me"* (Isaiah 6:8).

Your purpose is bigger than you think. Your purpose is greater than you can imagine. Some people act a certain way to sidetrack you or make you lose focus so that you place your eyes on their greatness or on their short comings. As a result, you become so over concerned about them and their issues that you lose sight of the ultimate and greater place that God is calling you to.

As leaders we can get so busy trying to get others in their place. Some of the people we are assiduously trying to pour into are not even concerned about the vision God has given to us. They are about their own agenda. You keep trying to fix them. You know what I am talking about, praying, laying hands, speaking prophetically into their lives and then it seems like they turn again to their vomit or betray you. Moreover, they refuse to eat at the Kings table. They insist on just settling for the crumbs from the table. I am here to provoke you to move beyond that. Grab a hold of the next dimension to your vision and, or your life. Don't let their lack of caring block, stifle or hinder you, *"Awake to Your Destiny!"*

It was just this week ending June 08, 2013, God spoke clearly to me, "take your mind off this and that and go all the way in". *"There is more I want to reveal to you, there is greater yet I want to pour out in you and through you"*. Immediately, my response was yes. I felt like a veil was rent. That same week the "Prophetic in Warfare Blog Radio was birth out and launched on June 13, 2013 (www.blogtalkradio.com/propheticinwarfare). That very week also, the Blog post website took off as well all on the same heading "Prophetic in Warfare" (http://www.apostlenadinemanning.wordpress.com).

Reflections

The question is what is your King Uzziah?-

_____

_____

_____

_____

_____

The other question is, what will it take for you to "Awake to your Destiny"?

_____

_____

_____

_____

_____

What is your commitment to move forward into your destiny and/or [your next assignment]?

_____

_____

_____

_____

_____

Chapter 5

Let the Word Work

What is it that God is calling you to do? Have you grown comfortable with everyday happenings and have become satisfied with circumstances that surround your life. Well I declare to you this day, "**Let the Word of God work.**"

Hebrews 4:12 declares,

"For the word of God is quick, and powerful, and sharper than any two-edged sword, piercing even to the dividing asunder of soul and spirit, and of the joints and marrow, and is a discerner of the thoughts and intents of the heart".

When you are bombarded with various trials remember that God has not forgotten you, He knows your name. Your trials and tribulation is to prove His character inside of you. The God who created something out of nothing comes to tell you that the same power that spoke *"Let there be light"* and there was light is still here today (Genesis 1:1-3).

44

St. John 1:1-5 says,

"In the beginning was the Word, and the Word was with God, and the Word was God. 2 The same was in the beginning with God. 3 All things were made by him; and without him was not anything made that was made. 4 In him was life; and the life was the light of men. 5 And the light shineth in darkness; and the darkness comprehended it not".

As our own words explain our minds to others, so was the Son of God sent in order to reveal his Father's mind to the world. Genesis chapter one reveals that, at the beginning of creation (the universe) the Word of God was at work. God spoke and it was done. Psalm 33:9 *"For he spoke, and it was done; he commanded, and it came into being"* [Jubilee]. He sent the Son of God in the form of man in order to reveal his Father's mind to the world. That power lives within according to St. John 1:12. You have the power to change the course of your destiny to align itself to God's divine plan by speaking it and it shall be done, by commanding this to come into manifestation and it shall be established. You have been anointed for [this] your destiny.

Do not become satisfied or comfortable with just enough, when the Lord is calling you into a place of true spiritual abundance. Don't allow someone else's success to hinder you our block your mind from seeing the full view of your destiny. Better yet, don't allow someone else lack of care or passion for the things of God hinder you from experiencing the "GLORY". Romans 8:22 declares that, *"For we know that the whole creation groaneth and travaileth in pain together until now."* The world is in travail, groaning for deliverance. The world in travail is certain; There is unrest and crying for deliverance everywhere. You may not understand its trouble, nor even what it wants, but its wishes are frustrated, and it is sighing for deliverance.

There is a nation awaiting their deliverance, crying out for you to be awaken to your destiny so they can be healed, delivered and set free. To fully comprehend your divine purpose and destiny you need to understand that your mind is the seat of understanding. You must grasp the revelation from Ephesians 2:6-7, *"and hath raised us up together, and made us sit together in heavenly places in Christ Jesus: 7 that in the ages to come he might shew the exceeding riches of his grace in his kindness toward us through Christ Jesus."*

My prayer for you my brothers and sisters in Christ is that you "**Awake to Your Destiny**" and that:

> *"The eyes of your understanding being enlightened; that ye may know what is the hope of his calling, and what the riches of the glory of his inheritance in the saints, 19 and what is the exceeding greatness of his power to us-ward who believe, according to the working of his mighty power "* (Ephesians 1:18-19).

Remember, there's nothing that is more powerful than a changed mind. Until your mind changes, you will repeat the same cycle over and over again.

What is it that God has impregnated your spirit with? What is it that you feel within you, as if having birthing pains as in child-birth. You find yourself many nights unable to sleep because the Spirit of the Lord has stirred your spirit and you are awaken, visualizing that thing with your eyes (spiritual eyes). I dare you to begin to prophesy, begin to make prophetic decrees and declaration in the spiritual realm that will activate your faith and release heavens divine intervention into your earthly situation.

These prophetic declaration works effectually as you push, travailing, and endeavoring to bring forth or birth the purpose that is within you. As you press through beyond the veil it releases the mind and will of the Lord for your life. Deliverance, healing, breakthrough and blessings are inevitable. This spiritual act of birthing is usually followed by prophetic instructions, revelation and or visions.

Be confident that your inheritance has been predestined and the Lord *"Worketh all things according to the counsel of His will"* (Ephesians 1:11b). It does not exempt you from spiritual warfare. In fact, it pushes you in a great place in the Lord. Yes, I know what God says in 2 Chronicles 20:17a-b" *You need not fight in this battle, Stand still and see the salvation of the Lord."* The Word of God to the army of Jehoshaphat is true. The battle is the Lord's, it is not a flesh and blood battle rather, it is a spiritual one. Your purpose and destiny cannot be thwarted no matter what evil Satan may bring.

The Word from the Lord through the prophet to the people was not for them to be still and do nothing. No, my friend, it was for them to activate their faith and believe God that this battle is already won in the Spirit. What He wanted them to do is stand on the Word of God and "*Let the Word Work*". As the army of Jehoshaphat positioned themselves for battle, further instructions came from the Lord saying

"Hear me, O Judah, and ye inhabitants of Jerusalem; Believe in the Lord your God, so shall ye be established; believe his prophets, so shall ye prosper".

You must believe God regardless of how you feel and what it looks like. If you are watching via YouTube the telecast on the "Faith Factor" or reading this book then you are alive on purpose to live on purpose. Awake to your Destiny and release the "Faith Factor" to walk into your purpose and destiny in this season. Hebrews 11:1-3 declares:-

"Now faith is the substance of things hoped for, the evidence of things not seen. 2 For by it the elders obtained a good report. 3 Through faith we understand that the worlds were framed by the word of God, so that things which are seen were not made of things which do appear".

Faith always has been the mark of God's servants, from the beginning of the world. Where the principle of faith is planted by the regenerating Spirit of God, it will cause the truth to be received. As you hope in the Lord, believing "NOW" for what is yet to come there will be a manifestation. The "Faith Factor" is your confidence that God is able to do it and it is the object of our hope. It is a firm persuasion and expectation, that God will perform all He has promised to us in Christ.

The army of Jehoshaphat heard that the people whom they did not fight with when they passed through their land, has now plotted to invade them and take their blessings. This drove Jehoshaphat and the people to seek the Lord in prayer and fasting and bring God's Word back to Him in remembrance of His promises saying:-

> **2 Chronicles 20:10-11** *"And now, behold, the children of Ammon and Moab and Mount Seir, whom thou wouldest not let Israel invade, when they came out of the land of Egypt, but they turned from them, and destroyed them not; 11* **Moreover, Jehoshaphat declared in prayer,** *"Behold, I say, how they reward us, to come to cast us out of thy possession, which thou hast given us to inherit".*

Moreover, Jehoshaphat recognized that worship was essential to release that Word of faith, they received from the Lord. Jehoshaphat prayed:-

> *"And in thine hand is there not power and might, so that none is able to withstand thee? 7 Art not thou our God, who didst drive out the inhabitants of*

this land before thy people Israel, and gavest it to the seed of Abraham thy friend forever? 8 And they dwelt therein, and have built thee a sanctuary therein for thy name, saying, 9 If, when evil cometh upon us, as the sword, judgment, or pestilence, or famine, we stand before this house, and in thy presence, (for thy name is in this house,) and cry unto thee in our affliction, then thou wilt hear and help" (2 Chronicles 20:6b – 9).

Jehoshaphat was establishing the fact that, Lord we have placed you first in all things. We have built a sanctuary in your name to worship you. Jehoshaphat was allowing the Word of God to work as he establishes in the realm of the spirit by his prophetic declaration that God was obligated to act because they created an atmosphere for Him to come and see about them.

Have you created a place and an atmosphere through worship for the manifestation of His Glory? It is the Word of God in you that ignites you to a place of continuous worship to be *"Awakened to Your Destiny"*! So I implore you, *"Let the Word Work"* in your life, because it is your assurance for blessings, healing and deliverance. The key to letting the

Word of God work is written in the book of St. John 15:7 *"If ye abide in me, and my words abide in you, ye shall ask what ye will, and it shall be done unto you"*. *"Let The Word Work"* in the name of Jesus.

You have it within you, the power of our Lord and Savior to speak to situations and healing, deliverance and transformation will take place. The Word of the Lord is nigh you, in your mouth and in your heart. It is the word of faith preached to you as Romans 10 declares. Letting the Word work is confessing that which is in your heart, the Word of faith believing that you receive it and it shall be done. Work that power within you. You have it in you, *"Let the Word Work"*.

Chapter 6

Submission to Christ

"Let this mind be in you which is also in Christ Jesus, who being in the form of God, did not consider it robbery to be equal with God", but made Himself of no reputation, taking the form of a bondservant, and coming in the likeness of men" (Philippians 2:5).

In order for us to have the mind of Christ and let the mind of Christ be in us we must submit ourselves to God. We cannot be high-minded, thinking that we don't need help, and we know it all. Jesus was willing to give up His rights to obey God and serve people. Therefore, like Christ we should have a willing heart to serve. A servant's heart has their mind set on serving out of love for God and others, not out of guilt and fear.

Obedience in serving comes from abiding in the Word of the Lord [John 15:1-8]. The mind becomes transformed as it is renewed day by day in the Word of the Lord. It was clear as Jesus taught His disciples that ultimately He wanted them to understand that being a follower of

Christ means denying yourself, take up the cross daily and follow Him, "I Surrender All." God is calling His church back to rebirth and re-kindle their passion for Him.

Cultivating God's Abiding Presence

> *"1 I am the true vine, and my Father is the husbandman. 2 Every branch in me that beareth not fruit he taketh away: and every branch that beareth fruit, he purgeth it, that it may bring forth more fruit. 3 Now ye are clean through the word which I have spoken unto you. 4 Abide in me, and I in you. As the branch cannot bear fruit of itself, except it abide in the vine; no more can ye, except ye abide in me"* (St. John 15:1-4).

God's people are viewed here as originating from Christ, organically united to Him, as branches emanating from the vine—the entire economy being under the care of the Father, the Vinedresser. The union between the vine and the branches is characterized by the expressions "in me" and "in you." The rebellious, disobedient spirit was engrafted in us through our old adamic nature, [carnal man] inherited from our forefathers.

The nation of Israel was birth out of the Patriarch Israel that tried to walk in their own way, yet the promises of God was theirs. You are already blessed. This has been pre-destined by God, all He want us to do is to come out of the mentality of Egypt and worship Him in Spirit and in truth.

The Israelites were in bondage in Egypt and God heard their cry and sent a deliverer in His name to deliver them. The promise was established through Abraham to rest on us who have been engrafted into the family tree of God (Gentiles through the shed blood of Jesus Christ).

> *"Through Christ Jesus, God has blessed the Gentiles with the same blessing he promised to Abraham, so that we who are believers might receive the promised* Holy Spirit through faith".* (Galatians 3:14).

God is gracious that His word guide us into all truth to free our mind and our spirit from bondage if we submit to Him. As we abide in Him, He reveals the things that need to be pruned from us. When you abide in Him He shows you where you miss the mark. As we yield ourselves to Christ, wherever we fall short and miss the mark the Word of God helps us identify where we are drifting away from God and draw us back to Him.

Why is God speaking to us as a community of believers to "Awake to Our Destiny"? This is because we have gotten accustomed to rituals. We know how to mask off what we are feeling inside: - the hurts, pain, jealousies, anger, rage, malice and so on. Even, fivefold leader's battle with these issues. Yes they do, they grew up in a traditional church, where you are only told what to do, how to do a certain way. Hence, you have grown comfortable with doing church because you know what it means to be saved. Abraham was called from what we describe as just saving station, a place of comfort into greater blessings and a greater God experience (Genesis 12).

> *"1 The Lord had said to Abram, "Leave your native country, your relatives, and your father's family, and go to the land that I will show you. 2 I will make you into a great nation. I will bless you and make you famous, and you will be a blessing to others. 3 I will bless those who bless you and curse those who treat you with contempt. All the families on earth will be blessed through you." 4 so Abram departed as the Lord had instructed"* (Genesis 12: 1-4).

You now understand that God is love. But there is more to the Kingdom than just sitting in the pews. There is a greater deliverance awaiting you. There is a greater purpose inside of you and God is calling you out of your comfort zone. It is when you shift in faith, surrendering to the will of the Lord for your life that your mind is transformed and you are released into a covenant relationship with God.

It is a personal relationship with the Lord that awakes and ignites you to think on purpose. As you begin to earnestly and eagerly seek the Lord you will realize there is something missing from "me". Who am I, what is my purpose and where am I going. There is more to "me" than just this. But first God wants to prune and purge away from us everything that has been twisted in our mind concerning the ministry of Jesus Christ.

What Have You Done With Jesus

The Lord revealed to me few months ago that while He was on earth doing the will of the Father with signs and wonders following Him that as He was teaching His disciples and spreading the Love of God in the community, the main purpose was to transform the thinking of those who followed Him. He was trying to enlighten the disciples and those who seek after Him for a special touch to the divine nature of supernatural realm. His goal was to open up their understanding about the Kingdom of God so they can walk in the power of the Spirit with a kingdom mentality or mindset.

Yet, the disciples marveled at some of the works that Christ did. Some faith waivered, some questioned His apostolic acts and why or who He was at the time. Jesus spoke many parables to them. Even though they were illustrated in a natural sense the parables had a heavenly meaning. His whole intent was to transform their mind and thinking to that of the Kingdom of heaven. God have given us these keys. In St. Matthew 16: 13-16 Jesus ask His disciples whom do men say I am and who do you say I am.

13b Whom do men say that I the Son of man am? 14 And they said, some say

that thou art John the Baptist: some,
Elias; and others, Jeremias, or one of the
prophets. 15 He saith unto them, But
whom say ye that I am? 16 And Simon
Peter answered and said, Thou art the
Christ, the Son of the living God
(Matthew 16:13b-16).

Many have their opinion of who Jesus was. Some say He was John the Baptist, some say Elijah, others say Jeremiah and some say the prophets. Peter understood who Jesus was because of divine revelation. He answered saying, *"You are the Messiah, the Son of the living God"* (Matthew 16: 16). Peter knew the truth because God revealed it to him. The other disciples were responding from a common view but Peter's response was a divine response, with confidence that Jesus Christ is the divine promise and long awaiting Messiah. He is our leader, defender and Savior.

There was a range of opinions given in Matthew 16:13-14, revealing that though all viewed Jesus as special, there were few who did not view Him as a truly unique individual, being the Son of God. But Peter's confession revealed that Jesus was a unique individual, Matthew 16:15-17.

13b Whom do men say that I the Son of man am? 14 And they said, some say that thou art John the Baptist: some, Elias; and others, Jeremias, or one of the prophets. 15 He saith unto them, But whom say ye that I am? 16 And Simon Peter answered and said, Thou art the Christ, the Son of the living God (Matthew 16:13b-16).

This chapter also reveals Jesus affirmation of that confession, the supernatural revelation from the Father and the divine connection that Jesus has to the Father (God). We need to awake to thinking with a mind transformed by divine revelation. When John received the awakening revelation about the churches in Revelation he was caught up into the supernatural realm when God commanded Him to *"come up hither".* 1 Corinthians 2:14 *"But the natural man receives not the things of the Spirit of God: for they are foolishness to him: neither can he know them, because they are spiritually discerned".*

Our minds must be transformed to think upon Jesus as our rock. He is the rock of the church. He calls us to a perpetual relationship and covenant with Him as Hebrew 8:10 explains:-

"For this is the covenant that I will make with the house of Israel after those days, says the LORD: I will put My laws in their mind and write them on their hearts; and I will be their God, and they shall be My people".

When our hearts are changed, following God's principles of the Kingdom will become a lifestyle. It will not be difficult or unpleasant because you are yielded to the Holy Spirit and He gives you new desires.

As we submit ourselves to the Holy Spirit, He gives us the innate desire to obey Christ. When Jesus Christ gave His life for us, was crucified, died, buried and rose again on the third day, it happened so that we might have life and life more abundantly. St. John 1:14, explains that the *"Word became flesh and dwelt among us".* Moreover, verse 12 reveals that *"as many have received Him to them gave ye power to become the Sons of God, even to them that believe on His name".*

Therefore, when God spoke to Peter in St. Matthew 19:18 saying that, *"That thou art Peter, and upon this rock I will build my church; and the gates of hell shall not prevail against it".* He is revealing to us that the rock on which the church is built is Jesus Himself as well as His work of salvation by dying for us on the cross. In addition to that, it also point out Peter as a great leader and a rock of the church. The above scripture verses reveals Christ true identity as the rock and Peters' identity and role in the church.

Through this revelation, God is saying to us, wake up to your true identity and spiritual position of authority that was invested in you through Jesus Christ. They tried and successfully killed our Lord and Savior, Jesus Christ. But the crucifixion of our Lord was ultimately was a part of God's redemption plan. A plan executed by God's divine order, predestined before the foundation of this world that He may live again through us and in us.

Your Purpose was Predestinated

The book of Ephesians chapter one explains explicitly that your destiny was already predestinated by God.

> *"Long before he laid down earth's foundations, he had us in mind, had settled on us as the focus of his love, to be made whole and holy by his love. Long, long ago he decided to adopt us into his family through Jesus Christ. (What pleasure he took in planning this!) He wanted us to enter into the*

celebration of his lavish gift-giving by the hand of his beloved Son" (Ephesians 1:4-6, The Message).

"It's in Christ that we find out who we are and what we are living for. Long before we first heard of Christ and got our hopes up, he had his eye on us, had designs on us for glorious living, part of the overall purpose he is working out in everything and everyone.
13-14 It's in Christ that you, once you heard the truth and believed it (this Message of your salvation), found yourselves home free—signed, sealed, and delivered by the Holy Spirit. This signet from God is the first installment on what's coming, a reminder that we'll get everything God has planned for us, a praising and glorious life.
(Ephesians 1:11-14, The Message).

Our divine destiny occurred through Jesus Christ sacrificial death. It was only through His sacrifice on our behalf that brought us into the privilege of being adopted and joint-heirs to the throne of grace. It was God's unchanging plan from the beginning that we develop *the "Mind of Christ"*, his nature through a personal

relationship with Him. Ephesians 1:11-12
confirms this saying"-

> *"In whom also we have obtained an inheritance, being predestinated according to the purpose of him who worketh all things after the counsel of his own will: 12 that we should be to the praise of his glory, who first trusted in Christ."*

God chose you and when He looks at you He sees you through His Spiritual eyes. Remember His ways are higher than our ways and His thoughts are higher than our thoughts. So when God looks at you, He sees you holy and blameless, as if you never sinned. You responsibility is to demonstrate the mind and an attitude of a holy behavior, ready to do His will.

All He wanted the Israelites to do in the book of Exodus was to *"Awake to Your Destiny – With the Mind of Christ".* When He sent Moses to deliver them, it was because He heard their cry for help. He never judged them according to their sins but mercifully pardon them. He sent His word of assurance of blessing and the purpose to which they were called. Deuteronomy 7:6-9 says,

> *"The Lord did not set his heart on you and choose you because you were more*

numerous than other nations, for you were the smallest of all nations!
8 Rather, it was simply that the Lord loves you, and he was keeping the oath he had sworn to your ancestors. That is why the Lord rescued you with such a strong hand from your slavery and from the oppressive hand of Pharaoh, king of Egypt. 9 Understand, therefore, that the Lord your God is indeed God. He is the faithful God who keeps his covenant for a thousand generations and lavishes his unfailing love on those who love him and obey his commands".

Just as He chose the nation of Israel and called them out to fulfil that which He had promised their ancestors. Likewise, He has chosen us as daughters and sons (believers) of the most high God. We are God's peculiar treasures to fulfil His mandate here on earth. Awake to your destiny, knowing that God's plan for your life cannot be thwarted, no matter what evil plots Satan throws at you.

Christ, who has become the chief cornerstone, the rock of the church can only be seen and re-birth through a remnant who will come alive (awake to their destiny) and let the Kingdom of God manifest through their lives.

The world is waiting for the manifestation of the sons of God.

We have been commissioned on the earth to reveal the glory of the Lord. The rebirth and regenerative Spirit of Christ must manifest through us to change the world, and the people around us. We are the foundation of Christ Kingdom here on earth. We are walking as common people just talking about the works that He has done, revealed in His word but we are yet to manifest the power of the Lord that 2 Corinthians 4:7 reveals saying ***"But we have this treasure in earthen vessels, that the excellency of the power may be of God, and not of us."***

Jesus posed these questions to His disciples after crying out to God in prayer, knowing that His death was drawing near he wanted to hear from His *disciples **"Whom do men say that I the Son of man am?"*** The question to you is the same right now, "**Whom do you say Jesus is**?" Don't sit around with the skeptics trying to question or argue the things of the spirit. Don't just get stuck in traditions how to be baptized and which day to worship. Jesus Christ came to redeem us from the curse of the law. We are alive as believers for one reason and is to rebirth the supernatural power of Jesus Christ in the earth.

The Pharisees carefully followed their religious rules and traditions, believing that this was the way to God. They also believed in the authority of all Scripture and in the resurrection of the dead. The Sadducees accepted only the books of Moses as Scripture and did not believe in life after death. In Jesus, however, these two groups had a common enemy, and they joined forces to try to kill Him. We have one common enemy and that is Satan. We must resist the devil and he will flee from us.

> *"7 So humble yourselves before God. Resist the devil, and he will flee from you. 8 Come close to God, and God will come close to you. Wash your hands, you sinners; purify your hearts, for your loyalty is divided between God and the world. 9 Let there be tears for what you have done. Let there be sorrow and deep grief. Let there be sadness instead of laughter, and gloom instead of joy. 10 Humble yourselves before the Lord, and he will lift you up in honor"* (James 4:7-10).

It is a submitted life to Christ that hears and responds to the Word of the Lord. It is a life that has been transformed and empowered that is able to resist the devils schemes and plans.

James 4:8 says, *"Come close to God and God will come close to you"*. This means that you should humble yourself under the mighty hand the Lord, yield yourself to His authority, His divine will, commit your life to His control and be willing to follow Him. This gives you the power and ability to resist the devil and he will flee from you. Don't allow Satan to entice you to sin, purify your heart (separate yourself) from the pride of life, lust of the eyes and flesh.

When you are totally submitted to God it results in a heart purged from worldliness. Hence, you are more spiritually alert and awaken to your destiny. As a result of this, there will be no room for double standard. As the scripture says, a double-minded man is unstable in all his ways.

What have you done with the keys given to you? You have been given the authority to bind and loose.

> *"18 Verily I say unto you, whatsoever ye shall bind on earth shall be bound in heaven: and whatsoever ye shall loose on earth shall be loosed in heaven. 19 Again I say unto you, that if two of you shall agree on earth as touching anything that they shall ask, it shall be done for them of my Father which is in heaven. 20 For where two or three are*

gathered together in my name, there am I in the midst of them." (Matthew 18:18-20).

What have you done with Jesus? We have been so busy trying to be doctrinal correct as a church. Busy trying to compete with each other. The Lord is saying to us, *"to stop all this contention"*. The hair splitting theories must be dropped and come together **"touching anything that they (we) shall ask, it shall be done for them (us) of my Father which is in Heaven. For where two or three are gathered together in my name, there I am in the midst"** (Matthew 18:19b-20). Awake to your destiny and live to declare the works of the Lord. He implores us today to strengthen ourselves in Him because *"Thou art the rock"*...and the gates of hell shall not prevail against you. The power of God is available to you through Jesus Christ. As Matthew 16:19 declares **"and I will give unto thee the keys of the kingdom of heaven: and whatsoever thou shalt bind on earth shall be bound in heaven: and whatsoever thou shalt loose on earth shall be loosed in heaven."**

Chapter 7

I Am Chosen

The laws written in the Old Testament point us to the new covenant received through the shed blood of Jesus Christ. Galatians 3 reveals to us *"Christ redeemed us from the curse of the law being made a curse for us. That the blessings of Abraham may rest on the gentiles through Jesus Christ"*. The revelation of who we are can only come through the Word of God and the Holy Spirit. St. John 16:16 declares that, *"You did not choose Me, but I chose you and appointed you that you should bear fruit, and that your fruit should remain, that whatever you ask the Father in My name He may give you"*.

Chosen means you have been selected, or preferred. Chosen is defined by scriptural reference that you have been predestined. You have been appointed by God to walk like Him and talk like Him. He gave a command saying,

"Let us make man into our image, after our likeness: and let them have dominion over the fish of the sea, and over the fowl of the air, and over the cattle, and over all the

earth, and over every creeping thing that creepeth upon the earth" (Genesis 1:26).

God wanted a replica of Himself in the earth. He originally made man from what had no life (dust), and said now live. God breathe the breath of His life into man and said now think like me. God says to you today, *"I have given you the mind of Christ, the wisdom and the counsel of God; The authority invested in Me has been given to you."*

> *"Then God blessed them and said, "Be fruitful and multiply. Fill the earth and govern it. Reign over the fish in the sea, the birds in the sky, and all the animals that scurry along the ground." 29 Then God said, "Look! I have given you every seed-bearing plant throughout the earth and all the fruit trees for your food. 30 And I have given every green plant as food for all the wild animals, the birds in the sky, and the small animals that scurry along the ground— everything that has life." And that is what happened"* (Genesis 1:28-29).

God needed someone to manage the things He established in the earth, to teach, instruct and to take dominion over everything He placed on the earth. It was Satan that beguiled Eve, who then enticed Adam to eat the forbidden fruit that brought sin upon the earth. But God in His grace and mercy sent to us salvation through the shed blood of Jesus Christ. His ultimate goal was to redeem man so that they can be awaken from dead works of the flesh and walk as children of light. *"God is light"*, means that God is perfectly holy and true and that He alone can guide us out of the darkness of sin.

Light is also related to truth in that light exposes whatever exists, whether it is good or bad. In the dark, good and evil look alike. In the light, they can be clearly distinguished. Just as darkness cannot exist in the presence of light, sin cannot exist in the presence of a holy God. If you want to have a relationship with God, choose to put aside any and all sinful ways of living. Having or developing the mind of Christ requires walking as children of the light. Before Adam and Eve sinned they had great peace and joy. They were sinless until the serpent beguiled Eve, who then enticed Adam to that sin of disobedience from God's original plan.

I Believe God

In 1 John 1:3-4, John reveals that first, our fellowship is grounded in the testimony of God's Word and is renewed daily by the Holy Spirit.

You are chosen by God, regardless of the situation before you, hold on to the profession of your faith without wavering. Hebrews 10:23 admonishes us, *"Let us hold fast the profession of our faith without wavering; (for he is faithful that promised)."*

In the initial stage of walking with Christ you may not have a complete understanding of who you are and what your purpose is. Nevertheless, you have personal access to God through Christ and as you draw near to Him you will grow in faith. Through a constant abiding relationship with Christ, your faith continues to grow. As your faith grows you overcome doubts and questions as your relationship deepens with God.

Your understanding inevitably becomes enlightened to the hope of your calling and you will ultimately emerge into your destiny. God establishes the promises and He is faithful *"who worketh all things according to the counsel of His will"* (Ephesians 1:11b). Holding on to the profession of our faith is believing and having the confidence that what God has promised it will come to pass. Philippians 1:6 declares, *"being confident of this very thing, that he which hath begun a good work in you will perform it until the day of Jesus Christ:"*

Hannah choose to remain God conscious, regardless of the obstacles that stood in her way. She had to believe God regardless of how it felt or what it looked like. She had to endure the provocation and ridicule of her adversary Peninnah. In the midst of her setback and adversity, it was her confidence and tenacity in God that kept her. She had developed the mind of Christ through enduring the difficult test of her faith.

It was the Lord that had shut up Hannah's womb according to 1 Samuel 1:5b. Even though her adversary mocked her, she persevered, continually worshipped the Lord and remained submissive to her husband and the priest of the temple Eli. Her destiny was in view and she had no energy to waste arguing with Peninnah. I hear the Lord say to you: "Don't be distracted".

David had some inclination about his purpose that he was anointed for the task because when the bears or lion came to attack the sheep he rose up to defend them by tearing the bear apart. While he was tending to the sheep on the backside of the desert, God was setting the stage for his destiny. He was doing the little things or menial task while his brothers went to war. He kept his mind stayed on the Lord, exalting God with high praises and encouraging himself in God even during his wilderness seasons.

When the Philistines threatened Israel, they were afraid. But David went fully armed with the Word of God as his armor and his faith in God. He had some good days and some bad days. For instance, when he had to contend with Goliath and even sought refuge from Saul who tried to kill him. David stayed awaken and alert, encouraging himself that *"it is in me to possess the gates of the enemy. It is in me to succeed."* I declare to you that you have been chosen to do greater works. I decree it is in you to succeed and it is in you to achieve in Jesus name.

As mentioned before in Chapter 6, Jesus purpose on earth was to teach His disciples and transform their mind to that of the principles of the Kingdom. Jesus carefully selected His disciples. Even though, they had their fears, shortcomings and some doubts He never gave up on them. God is speaking to you from these pages to arise and strengthen the things that remain. Don't give up on God for He won't give up on you...He's able!

You may have given up on your purpose, vision, ministry, children or even believing in yourself or God. There are a few also, reading this page that have gotten discouraged because you shared your dreams with someone who told you that it was not possible. Maybe you wanted validation from your leader or someone you looked up to move into your destiny. You may have even gotten discouraged to the point where you begin to spend your time money and service doing something that does not maximize your potential.

I decree and declare that now is your set time of favor. You must stay the course and believe God. If He purpose it, shall He not do it? God is not a God to lie, *"Believe in the Lord your God, so shall ye be established; believe his prophets, so shall ye prosper"* (2 Chronicles 20:20).

From Perseverance to Progression

Perseverance means determination, persistency or diligence. The question is how bad to you want it? How determined are you to walk into your destiny? Whatever you desire from the Lord you must seek after it. Hannah persevered, she was determined to birth out the "prophetic" that was inside of her. When your purpose is extraordinary, beyond the norm of religious status quo you have to shift from just perseverance to progression. Progression means headway, advancement or development.

A woman can naturally give birth to a child or it can be done by C-Section. C-Section is a quick process involving cutting or making an incision in the abdomen and remove the fetus. But when a woman in labor travail, feels the pain and push, and keep on pushing, she is making headway or advancement into a wonderful experience of giving birth to something precious. It is a feeling of endurance and perseverance to a place where you can't hold back, or be still or else the baby will die. She has to place effort and press forward with all her might and with all her strength.

Hannah's determination turned her trial into triumph and she birthed out an Apostolic voice to the nation (Samuel). What is inside of you is for signs, wonders and miracles in this season. Don't just persevere, be progressive and press, push and move forward into your destiny. Keep your eyes on the prize and like Hannah turn your pain in to praise. Her constant fellowship and perseverance help her to progress to a place in the spiritual realm in (Shiloh) which allowed her to birth out her destiny. Your praise releases your faith into the throne room of heaven where progression (birthing) takes place.

Chosen to Bear Fruit

But you have to be honest, open and humble before the Lord. He is saying to you my daughter or my son:-

> *"Ho! Everyone who thirsts, Come to the waters; and you who have no money, Come, buy and eat. Yes, come, buy wine and milk; without money and without price. 2 Why do you spend*

money for what is not bread, and your wages for what does not satisfy? Listen carefully to Me, and eat what is good, and let your soul delight itself in abundance. 3 Incline your ear, and come to Me. Hear, and your soul shall live; and I will make an everlasting covenant with you. The sure mercies of David. 4 Indeed I have given him as a witness to the people" (Isaiah 55:1-4).

As you pursue the Lord with all your heart He will give you the desires of your heart. He knew there was some good works that the church in Sardis did but they became inconsistent with their pursuit after God. They started rationalizing everything according to the patterns of the world system. God doesn't want us to just persevere put He wants us to progress. This can only take place when our mind is transformed through His word and we begin do things as we are led by the Holy Spirit.

We have gotten so accustomed to making our own decisions, even in the midst of all the economic changes taking place. We make our decisions then bring them to God. Not having a full-time job for over three (3) years my faith was tested to trust the Lord in a new dimension. Even though, I have seen and encountered great deliverances and miracles through the ministering of God's word prophetically over the past five (5) years the Lord was preparing me to take on a greater assignment that would require me to think like Him with "THE MIND OF CHRIST."

The Lord was calling me to the ministry of pastoral and it would take stepping out by faith, with no fulltime job, four (4) children and a husband. I was studying full-time, nonetheless, I heard the Lord say this is your season this is your time. God is calling us to "Awake to Our Destiny" not because of our successes or triumphs like the people in Sardis who had it good. The Lord is calling us back to a place of brokenness where He becomes the center of our joy and not our jobs, our husbands, children or "the church". He is saying awake to your destiny and strengthen the things that remain.

Many leaders and members right now are experiencing a drought in their ministry, many have left the ministry because they are burnt out and have lost their flavor with God because of trials. Some are too busy making money they say to keep bread on the table. Yet, there is still not enough even though you try hard to fix it. God is saying to us His chosen people, *"come and chase after to me, only I can quench the deep thirst and longing in your soul."*

I hear the Spirit of the Lord bidding you to come closer to Him. He wants to heal you, He wants to touch you and reveal more to you, greater things than you can ever imagine.

> *"Is anyone thirsty? Come and drink—even if you have no money! Come, take your choice of wine or milk—it's all free! 2 Why spend your money on food that does not give you strength? Why pay for food that does you no good? Listen to me, and you will eat what is good. You will enjoy the finest food. 3 "Come to me with your ears wide open. Listen, and you will find life. I will make an everlasting covenant with you. I will give you all the unfailing love I promised to David"* (Isaiah 55:1-3).

There are some that are faithfully serving in the church but have lost their pursuit of passion for Christ. You have settled for just church as usual and God is calling you to a deeper place in Him where you are totally immersed in His glory. Elijah had many triumphs, yet he ran into hiding when His life was threatened by Jezebel. He felt lonely, afraid and discouraged. But I admired one thing about this great man, he went to find God in the midst of his dilemma.

Great writers speak about his weaknesses and there are great theologians who argue and write awesome commentaries on Elijah's fear. But do you see what I see, or hear what I hear. He exposed himself to God. He choose to abide in Him and open up to let God know what his fears were. From this scenario of Elijah fears and discouragement we are reminded that

> *"Every branch in me that beareth not fruit he taketh away: and every branch that beareth fruit, he purgeth it, that it may bring forth more fruit"* (St. John 15:2). While in the presence of the Lord he gained new strength to arise for the next assignment.

Christ, The Vine Manager

Christ is the vine manager and we are the branch in Him the vine. The branches represent those who claim to be followers of Christ. You only bear fruit and become more fruitful as you remain in living union with Christ. It is a living relationship not a dead one. If you don't yield yourself to Him, no fruit can come forth. Have you ever planted some trees, flowers or seeds and it seem like for weeks, and months nothing coming forth, except for say one out of ten seeds that you planted or just a few blossoms sprung up and you had expected more.

Even years after planting a tree and nothing comes forth, you are tempted to just cut it down. Or maybe you became so discouraged you are ready to give up on those things you plan. The expectation from the number of seeds you planted seemed unresponsive to the nutrients given to it to sustain it.

> *"Here is another illustration Jesus used: "The Kingdom of Heaven is like a mustard seed planted in a field. 32 It is the smallest of all seeds, but it becomes the largest of garden plants; it grows into a tree, and birds come and make nests in its branches."* (Matthew 13:31).

Don't be discouraged by what you see in the natural. Remember, that the mustard seed was the smallest seed a farmer used. Jesus used this parable to show that the Kingdom has small beginnings but will grow and produce great results. Many leaders right now have gotten discouraged because they don't see the fruits they expected.

God is in the business of restoration, renewal, re-birth and revival and you will reap if you faint not. Forsake your will and yield yourself to God's will. As you submit to His will, your process of being shaped into a clearer picture of Christ [His image and likeness] gradually conforms you to the image of your predestinated purpose and position. Awake to your destiny, believe God, that He has chosen you, you have a place in history and that you are right for the part.

> *Thank you Lord that you are ready to do what you said you would do. Thank you Lord that you are prepared to complete what you promised according to Isaiah 62. Thank you that I am chosen. I am being confident of this very thing that that the work that you have begun in me will be completed in Jesus name.*

Chapter 8

Prophetic Prayer Declaration

Dear Heavenly Father, I thank you that in you I live, move and have my being. You said *"Those who remain in me, and I in them, will produce much fruit. For apart from me you can do nothing."*

I declare that there will be no more stagnation in my life. I decree that everything in me that does not bear fruit is purged from me right now and I am awakened to my destiny with the mind of Christ to bear fruit and the fruit will remain because I choose to live by your Word.

I decree and declare that I have been chosen by God to bear fruit, and the fruit shall remain (St. John 15:16). As the scripture says without you I can't do nothing.

I surrender my gifts, talents and will to your divine will and destiny for my life.

I have been chosen by God, I have a place in history, I am apart of those chosen to be used by God in the earth and I am right for the part. By the confession of my mouth because of a renewed mind in the Word of God that transformed by heart: - I am **"<u>Awaken to My Destiny</u>"** in Jesus name, Amen!

Apostolic Voice to the Nation

Apostle Nadine Manning

Chapter 9

Apostle Nadine Manning

Biography

Apostle Nadine Manning was born and raised in Spanish Town, Jamaica. She has been happily married for thirteen years to Pastor Richard Manning who is also a native of Jamaica. They are the proud parents of seven year old triplets Abigail, Aaron, and Nathaniel and five year old Joshua Manning; all a product of the miracles of prayer and prophetic intercession.

Apostle Nadine is the founder and owner of Genius Kids Academy & Learning Institute Inc., in Millville, NJ USA; a nonprofit agency which she envision to provide childcare for infants and toddlers, and before and afterschool care for school age children. Apostle Nadine and Pastor Richard Manning hold an Associate's Degree in Theology. Apostle Nadine holds degrees also Associates Degrees Business

Administration and Public Administration, and a Bachelor Degree in Business Management. Apostle Nadine is currently pursuing her Masters.

Apostle Nadine Manning has been ministering and operating in the office of a Prophet, Prophetic Renegade Worshipping Warrior and Evangelical Preacher and Teacher for over 15 years. She taught on Prophetic in Warfare at a theological college as well as ministering across Jamaica doing revivals and conferences with Remnant Ministries International. She has a passion for intercession and host a series of Prophetic Watch of the Lord services, teachings on the Ministry of the Watchman and Prophetic Intercession, The Priesthood of the Believer and more.

Apostle Nadine has a Global mandate to teach, train and release intercessors, worshippers and all kingdom ambassadors into their position as a Watchman. The Apostolic anointing on her life enable her to identify gifts in your life and speak a life changing word to catapult you into your purpose and release you into the next dimension. She has a great passion for intercession and standing in the gap for others and the nations to see lives change, souls saved and transformation takes place globally.

Almost two years ago, Apostle Nadine and Pastor Richard Manning was led of God to establish a church to show the love of God and to help the people in the community. Apostle Nadine and Pastor Richard Manning has a passion for winning souls for the body of Christ so that people will be healed and restored to their rightful place in God and walk into their divine destiny. Apostle Nadine and Pastor Richard Manning established Prophetic in Warfare Deliverance and Worship Tabernacle in March 2011 and officially opened the doors for church in June 2011 in Millville, New Jersey.

Prophetic in Warfare Deliverance and Worship Tabernacle is a 501(c) (3) nondenominational global ministry established for Kingdom Purpose and Assignment where signs and wonders and miracles are in the midst. Prophetic in Warfare Deliverance and Worship Tabernacle began in Jamaica as a teaching ministry. Apostle Nadine and Pastor Richard Manning want to help the people in the community who are hopeless, defeated, victims of abuse, and living in poverty.

The vision of Apostle Nadine and Pastor Richard Manning as Pastors and leaders of Prophetic in Warfare Deliverance and Worship Tabernacle is to enable people to be empowered and completely released to walk into their God-given purpose and assignment through the teaching and demonstration of God's Word and the unction of Holy Spirit, to advance the Kingdom of God in the earth preaching deliverance and setting the captives free, (Isaiah 61:1-6). It is the passion of Apostle Nadine and Pastor Richard Manning to increase the people's knowledge as it relates to the Prophetic Intercession, Spiritual Warfare, Deliverance and Worship.

- The mission of Prophetic in Warfare Deliverance and Worship Tabernacle is one of reconciliation, to spread the love of God and the way of Salvation through Jesus Christ to our community and as a Global initiative. In one year Apostle Nadine and Pastor Richard Manning have launched and hosted a series of prolific and prophetic triumphs for the Lord.

- On November 19 2011, within five (5) months in ministry they launched and hosted the first "The Ingathering of God's Army" Prophetic Watch of the Lord Conference. A mandate by God calling all intercessors, worship leaders, and the fivefold ministers of the gospel with teachings on Prophetic Intercession, The Priesthood of the Believer, The Watchman Anointing, and Strategic Levels of Spiritual Warfare.

- On February 2, 2012 the Deborah's Daughter Company was launched to assemble a company of women who are willing to hear God's voice and obey his Word. This vision resulted in the launch of the Deborah's Daughter Company's YES Women's Conference and Revival that was held May 24-26, 2012.

- The Kingdom Troops Youth Fellowship was launched February

17, 2012 with a dynamic Black
History focus presentation.

- Apostle Nadine and Pastor Richard
  Manning launched the Prophetic
  Watch of the Lord Summit on
  February 25, 2012; where God's
  intercessors gathered to cry aloud
  and spear not and make prophetic
  decrees for their city, nation, and
  families and the global community.

- Since that time they now host a
  monthly "Prophetic Watch of the Lord
  –Glory Cloud Prayer." four (4) hours
  of none stop prayer, praise, and
  prophetic intercession as the people
  gather the Glory of the Lord
  descends in the midst like fog/cloud
  and the anointing with fire as they
  decree "we are going see what we
  been praying for!!!

- Lives are being changed through the
  prayer gatherings, instant healings, a
  spiritual release to a next dimension,
  families being restored, salvation
  coming to loved ones and souls
  coming into the kingdom. People
  have been traveling from Maryland,

Connecticut, New York, and Canada!! For the outpouring in the Glory Cloud Prayer Services!!!

- Apostle Nadine and Pastor Richard Manning recently went to Jamaica with a mandate by God calling all Parishes, Fivefold leaders, Prayer Warriors, Prophets, and Worshippers to gather together to take back Spanish Town and its environ for Jesus as a they hosted the Prophetic Watch of the Lord Summit -2 August 10-11, 2012.

- The mission of Prophetic in Warfare Deliverance and Worship Tabernacle is being fulfilled in Cumberland County, NJ through the community outreach programs from the Deborah's Daughters Company Ministries Inc. women's ministry and the Men with a Mission ministry.

- This is just the beginning of what is to come because they are destined for greatness. Without a doubt Apostle Nadine Manning and Pastor Richard Manning are "Awakened To Their Destiny".

References

Jenkins, Charles, 2010, *Thriving in Change.* Baxter Press (2010).

Life Application Bible, Tyndale House Publishers; Wheaton, Ill.: Tyndale House; Grand Rapids, Mich.: Zondervan Pub. House, 1991.

Dr. Myles Munroe; *The Power of Praise and Worship.* Destiny Image Publishers, 2000.

Vine, W. E., Unger, M. F., White, W., & Vine, W. E. (1985). *Vine's Complete Expository Dictionary of Old and New Testament words.* Nashville: Nelson.

Contact Us:

Apostle Nadine Manning Bookings for: - Conferences, Workshops, Revivals or Prophetic in Warfare Summit or Prayer Clinic at your church.

Please email us at propheticinwarfare@gmail.com or visit us on the web at: - www.globalpropheticinwarfareministries.com.

Mailing Address

Apostle Nadine Manning

P.O. Box 343, Millville New Jersey 08332

Follow Apostle Nadine on Twitter:

@ApostleNadine and/or @PropheticinWDWT or

Find encouragement and inspiration on Apostle Nadine Facebook Page

www.facebook.com/apostlenadineh.manning

Or her blog at:

www.Apostlenadinemanning.wordpress.com

www.ingramcontent.com/pod-product-compliance
Lightning Source LLC
Chambersburg PA
CBHW060134050426
42448CB00010B/2111